Dear Parents, Caregivers, and Educators:

This book presents everyday issues that all children face. On page 22, you'll find some questions to help children further explore these issues, both as they are presented in the story, and also as they might apply in the children's own lives. We hope these questions serve as starting points for developing a deeper understanding and appreciation of this book and the challenging situations it presents.

First American edition published in 2005 by
Picture Window Books
5115 Excelsior Boulevard
Suite 232
Minneapolis, MN 55416
877-845-8392
www.picturewindowbooks.com

First published in 2001 by
A & C Black (Publishers) Ltd
37 Soho Square
London WID 3QZ

Text copyright © Citizenship Foundation 2001
Illustrations copyright © Tim Archbold 2001

Published in conjunction with the
Citizenship Foundation.
Sponsored by British Telecom.

Printed in the United States of America.

Library of Congress Cataloging-in-Publication Data
Rose, Gill, 1949-
William and the guinea pig : a book about responsibility / by
Gill Rose ; illustrated by Tim Archbold.
p. cm. — (Making good choices)
Summary: William does not want his sister to spend time with
the guinea pig he received for his birthday, but later he finds a
reason to change his mind.
ISBN 1-4048-0664-4 (hardcover)
[1. Pets—Fiction. 2. Brothers and sisters—Fiction. 3.
Responsibility—Fiction. 4. Sharing—Fiction. 5. Guinea pigs—
Fiction.] I. Archbold, Tim, ill. II. Title. III. Series.
PZ7.R7157Wi 2004
[E]—dc22   2004007471

William and the Guinea Pig

by Gill Rose

illustrated by Tim Archbold

PICTURE WINDOW BOOKS
Minneapolis, Minnesota

The school had a new guinea pig.
William was thrilled when he was
allowed to hold the guinea pig.

Soon it would
be William's birthday.

"Please, please, can I have
a guinea pig of my own?"
he begged his mom.

"I'm sorry," said Mom, "but I won't have time to look after a guinea pig as well as work all day at the store."

"I'll look after it all by myself," promised William.
"You won't have to do anything."

"Well, all right then," said Mom.   5

When William woke up on his birthday, he was very excited.

Mom led him to the utility shed with Kelly, his little sister. William saw the brand-new hutch and rushed over to open the door.

There, sitting on a pile of straw, was the most beautiful golden-haired guinea pig.

"He's fantastic!" shouted William.
"I'm going to call him Sandy."

"Can I hold him, please, William?"
asked Kelly.

"No," said William.
"He's mine, and you're too young." 7

For the first few days, William spent
most of his spare time down in the shed
looking after Sandy.

He even forgot about playing soccer
with Rafiq, his best friend.

Every day, Kelly asked William
if she could help, but William
always said no.

"That's not fair," said Kelly.

"It's William's guinea pig,"
Mom said.
"If he says you can't help,
then you can't." 9

Kelly was mad at William for being so selfish.
Sometimes she sneaked into the shed
when he wasn't there, just to look at Sandy.
But she made sure Mom didn't see her.

On Saturday, William wanted to play soccer with
Rafiq. It had been a long time since their last game.

"You can go when you've cleaned
out Sandy's hutch," Mom said.

"I'll do it later, honest,"
said William.

A few days later, William and Kelly's cousin Rachel came to visit.

"Show Rachel your new guinea pig, William," said Mom.

Suddenly, William began to feel very bad. It had been days since he had checked on Sandy. He wondered what happens to a guinea pig that has not been fed.

"Can't I show her later?" he said.

"No, let's go now," Mom said, "before we have lunch."

As they walked toward the shed,
William felt his face getting
redder and redder. Mom would
be so angry with him.

"She might take Sandy
away from me," he thought.

But when they opened the door
of the shed, William had a big surprise.

There was Sandy, sitting happily in
his nice clean hutch. He had lots of food
in his bowl, and his bottle was full of water.

Sandy began to squeak as Kelly poked
some fresh leaves through the wire.
Then William knew who had been
looking after Sandy.

"Nice job, William," said Mom, smiling.
"You've been very good."

At bedtime, when Rachel had gone,
William found Kelly reading in bed.

"Thanks, Kelly," he said.
"I'm sorry I said you were too young
to help look after Sandy."

And from then on, they shared their
beautiful golden-haired guinea pig.

William and Kelly agreed that
it was a good idea to help each
other. And Rafiq was happy, too.   21

Something to think about ...

- Why do you think William wants a pet?

- What do you think a guinea pig needs for a happy, healthy life?

- Do you think William's mom was wrong to let William have a pet? Why do you think this?

- Was William's Mom right to trust William when he said he would look after Sandy? Why or why not?

- How would you describe William's behavior toward Sandy?

- When Kelly found out that William wasn't looking after Sandy, she began to do it herself secretly. Do you think that was the right thing to do?

- Do you think Kelly was right not to tell on William? Why or why not?

- William did not tell the truth when Mom said he had done a good job of looking after Sandy. What do you think about that?

- Kelly forgave William for what he had done. What does it mean to forgive someone? Is it easy to do? Why or why not?

- William and Kelly thought that helping each other look after Sandy was a good idea. Whom was it good for, and how?

Glossary

fantastic—terrific or wonderful

hutch—a cage for a small animal

selfish—only caring about yourself

utility—something useful

To Learn More

At the Library

Edgar, Kathy, Susan Edgar, and Joanne Mattern. *Responsibility.*
   Boston: Learning Challenge, 2003.

Nelson, Robin. *Being Responsible.* Minneapolis: Lerner
   Publications, 2003.

Loewen, Nancy. *Do I Have To? Kids Talk About Responsibility.*
   Minneapolis: Picture Window Books, 2003.

On the Web

FactHound offers a safe, fun way to find Web sites related to this book.
All of the sites on FactHound have been researched by our staff.
www.facthound.com

1. Visit the FactHound home page.
2. Enter a search word related to this book, or type in this special code: 1404806644.
3. Click the FETCH IT button.

Your trusty FactHound will fetch the best Web sites for you!

Look for all of the books in this series:

Joe's Car

The Sandbox

The Scary Movie

William and the Guinea Pig